S0-BUW-302

The Maps

by Mandy Peterson
illustrations by Joan Holub

Harcourt Brace & Company
Orlando Atlanta Austin Boston San Francisco Chicago Dallas New York Toronto London

"Rap, rap. Tap, tap."
Jan ran to see who was
rapping and tapping
at her door.

Jan found a map tacked
to her door! It said, "Find
the cap."

Jan ran with the map
and found the cap—and
another map. It said, "Find
the mat."

Jan ran with the maps and
the cap. Jan found the mat—
and another map. It said,
"Find the sack."

Jan ran with the maps, the cap, and the mat. Jan found the sack—and another map. It said, "Find the tan van."

Jan ran with the maps, the cap, the mat, and the sack. Jan found the tan van—and another map. It said, "Find the napping cat."

Jan ran with the maps, the
cap, the mat, the sack, and
the tan van. Jan found the
napping cat—and another
map. "Find the can."

Jan ran with the maps, the cap, the mat, the sack, the tan van, and the napping cat. Jan found the can—and another map. "Find the hat."

Jan ran with the maps, the cap, the mat, the sack, the tan van, the napping cat, and the can. Jan found the hat—and another map.

"I've had it!" Jan said. "I am going back home!"

But Jan WAS home!